How To Stay Out Of Jail - God's Way
By
Richard Okoronkwo

———————————

How to Stay Out of Jail – God's Way
By Richard Okoronkwo

Published By Parables
May, 2021

All Rights Reserved. No part of this book may be reproduced or utilized in any form or by any means, electronic or mechanical, including photocopying, **recording, or by any information storage and retrieval system, without permission in writing from the author. Unless otherwise noted, all Bible translations are drawn from the KJV and the NKJV translations of the Bible.**

      Printed in the United States of America

Readers should be aware that Internet Web sites offered as citations and/or sources for further information may have been changed or disappeared between the time this was written and the time it is read.

How To Stay Out Of Jail - God's Way

By
Richard Okoronkwo

FOREWORD

I want to thank my Lord Jesus for bringing me to a place where I understood that I needed to write this book. I thank Him for his revelation and invaluable insight that money cannot buy. I'm truly grateful as it has been a journey to get to this point. I'm writing this book by the inspiration of the Holy Spirit. I'm not smart enough to have this type of information. The spirit of God is talking while I'm writing for most of the book. It is not like a prophet who sees and writes but more of a knowing. Words pouring into me like a stream of water flowing nonstop. As long as it is running I can write all day but when it stops I have nothing to write. When it comes I'm writing fast enough trying to keep up. God is in control of this. He is the initiator and this book is coming from Him. Father God help me to do this right, to communicate exactly what you want written in Jesus' name Amen.

Table of Contents

- CHAPTER 1: I NEED GOD IN MY LIFE 1
- CHAPTER 2: GOD SPEAKS IN DIFFERENT WAYS 8
- CHAPTER 3: THE BIBLE 16
- CHAPTER 4: HELP ME STAY OUT OF JAIL 22
-     KNOW GOD FOR YOURSELF 23
- CHAPTER 5: CONTROL YOUR ANGER.................................30
- CHAPTER 6: LIFE IS NOT ABOUT BEING THE BEST.........36
- CHAPTER 7: HUMBLE YOURSELF 44
- CHAPTER 8: GOD'S TIME 50
- CHAPTER 9: REFUSE TO BE OFFENDED.............................59
- CHAPTER 10: PRACTICE HONESTY & INTEGRITY 68
- CHAPTER 11: IF YOU ARE IN JAIL......................................74
- CHAPTER 12: SHAME 82
- CHAPTER 13: STREET MENTALITY 90
- CHAPTER 14: READ THE BIBLE DAILY 104
- CHAPTER 15: DREAM DAILY 114
- CHAPTER 16: NOW THAT YOU ARE OUT OF JAIL 116
- CHAPTER 17: WHERE ARE YOU?......................................120
- CHAPTER 18: REFUSING COUNSEL 124
- CHAPTER 19: INTERCESSOR 128

CHAPTER 1: I NEED GOD IN MY LIFE

Our Father in heaven, Hallowed be Thy name, Thy kingdom come and Thy will be done on earth as it is in heaven. (Mathew 6:9-13). We are living in a time where people are forsaking the ways of God, chasing knowledge, insight and in some ways, becoming intellectuals. All of a sudden, they think they are smart and that they can explain humanity and the origin of man. A human being without God is a person in trouble. God created the heavens and the earth whether you believe it or not. For you and me to get to a place where we think we don't need God is an absolute joke. To be successful in the earth is to have carried out the plan of God for your life. It is the reason why He created you even in this generation. Your refusal to acknowledge and get to know Him is your way of abandoning His plan for your own. There is a problem with this. For you to have a successful plan, you would need to know the future. To have the ability to know what would happen tomorrow, next year and the rest of lifetime in advance to come up with a successful plan. It is only God who has that Ability. You can be successful according to the earth, or the world standard. However, you have failed in the sight of God because that was not why He created you. You made your plan. God made us for a specific reason and He is the only one that can reveal what that reason is. Make no mistake about it. The process of revealing that reason can be a very exhausting one. This is the reason why many quit without ever knowing why they are here. Only serious Christians know why they are here. Those who refuse to leave His presence will keep asking until He tells them. Your life starts the day you learn why God created you, and you begin to acknowledge God for who

He is. I'm speaking of the God of Abraham, Isaac & Israel. He can take you from the backside of the desert to become a king like David. Do you know that God is greater than man? If you can grasp that understanding, that you need Him every day to succeed, then you have started living. As you learn to trust Him, He will begin to show you things you cannot imagine. (1 Corinthians 2:9) KJV "But as it is written, Eye hath not seen, nor ear heard, neither have entered into the heart of man, the things which God hath prepared for them that love Him." Supernatural doors will begin to open for you. God is a supreme being, and He is powerful in all of his ways. He controls the air we breathe, the trees can understand Him when He speaks, and He gives instructions to the ocean. He is God all by Himself. He was not voted into power. He can take you from nowhere and make you somebody overnight.

Have you ever experienced the presence of God? It is the presence of a supernatural being who doesn't sleep nor slumber. He is the One who visits men made of flesh. If you ever experience His presence, no one could ever tell you that God is not real. There is something these believers know that you haven't felt. The power of His presence transforms you into the best version of yourself. So much so that you are staring at yourself, and you can't believe it's you. Believe it. God is amazing! If you don't know Him, you are missing out. It's like being on the wrong channel of a radio. You have to fix it. Receive Jesus as your Lord and personal Savior today by saying this simple prayer.

"Lord Jesus, today I come to you a sinner. Wash me with your blood and make me new again. I believe my sins are forgiven in Jesus' name. Amen".

That's it. You are a believer. Find a Bible-based church, and learn about Him. Also, learn how to apply His principles into your life. Welcome to the kingdom of God. To succeed in this life, according to the standard of heaven, you need to connect to the Master Planner, the Orchestrator of that plan, God. Each individual on earth has a specific instruction to help them succeed. No two are the same. Some plans seem similar, but still are not the same. The devil plots to destroy the plan God has for you by using different things to distract you from paying attention to God's ways. (Jeremiah 29:11) NIV. "For I know the plans I have for you," declares the LORD, "plans to prosper you and not to harm you, plans to give you hope and a future." Every plan God wrote for us has success written all over it. So the devil comes in to attempt to change it by deceiving us on the earth. He uses tricks we have never seen because he has been around for a very long time. He has tried different things and techniques all through different generations. He knows what worked on your parents and grandparents. You need God's help to defeat him, and to know about yourself. God will reveal what he wrote in His book about you. He will tell you what He put inside of you as a secret weapon to defeat the devil because He knew this day would come. "Then said I, Lo, I come: in the volume of the book it is written of me, I delight to do thy will, O my God: yea, thy law is within my heart." (Psalm 40:7-8) KJV.

God's plan for your life is already written. Will you follow God's plan or your own? You are free to do as you wish. Remember God will only back His plan. You are on your own with your plan. Angels have to read it to help you accomplish what is written of you. When you connect to God, it makes the angel's job easier in helping you.

CHAPTER 2: GOD SPEAKS IN DIFFERENT WAYS

The Bible tells us in (Job 33:14) "For God speaks once, yea twice, yet man perceives it not." As we continue to grow in God, it is important to learn the different ways that God speaks. In the church, we love when a prophet speaks to us to relate what God has said, but I tell you a mystery. As a believer, you become more effective when you learn how God speaks to you. He will speak to you through your supervisor at work, and He will speak through the guy on the street corner if you recognize it. He will speak through your wife, your daughter, son, etc. They won't always know it, but you will if you learn how to recognize God speaking to you. When you learn to serve God in this way, it removes limits from your life. He can reach you whenever He wants to. There will be more of a flow in your life concerning what God is doing in your life. He doesn't have to wait to speak through a prophet because that's the only way you understand Him to speak.

Do you know that God could speak just by the sun coming out, or a bird flying over your house? He will show you signs that mean a specific thing in your life. This is not diabolical. I will never forget many years ago, when God gave a word to a prophet to give me. He spoke it in a way that the prophet didn't have any idea what he was saying. He spoke through him to me in code. He gave me the message by saying in quote.

"The rainbow has come out but it only has Red, Orange and Green colors on it".

That was the message. The man of God was confused. He said to me, "I don't understand the message." And I said to him, "He didn't want you to know what He was saying to me. He wanted to know what it meant and I said to him, "It is not for you to know." Now about 5 months earlier, God was teaching me how He will speak by sending different colors of birds. In that season I wanted to see the birds every day, I would wake up, come outside, and see a different color every day. God was speaking without words or a voice but with symbols and animals. It was powerful. Today He's got me writing these mysteries because we have limited Him. We think that God only relates messages through the traditional way of prophecy or word of knowledge. No, God speaks through every minute and every second of the day. He can show you there is danger without words, and He can show you it's time to pray without visions. He is the almighty God and there is none like Him. Get Him out of box you've put Him in and learn the ways of God. Now, let's turn back to the quote.

"The rainbow has come out but it only shows Red, Orange and Green colors on it".

Red bird means good luck, Orange means excitement and bliss, and Green means adventure is in your future.

This means I'm bringing you good luck with excitement and adventure. If God made it, He can use it to speak or do whatever He wishes. "Noah sent out a raven to find dry land because of its strength of long flight and ability to feed on many different sources." (Gen. 8:7). Ravens fed Elijah when he was hiding from Ahab (1 Kgs. 17:4-6). ... "The ravens were appointed to bring him meat and did so."

Have you learned the ways of God? When the rainbow comes out, God is revealing to us that He is still keeping the covenant He made with Noah. This promise is that He will never destroy the earth with a flood. (Genesis 9:1-11). Not only did God set a rainbow in the clouds as a sign to Noah, he also promised the rainbow as a reminder of this covenant between Himself and Man. God is interested in you. You have tendencies and habits that He built inside of you when He made you. These tendencies and habits are there to respond to your destiny needs. You will need His help to navigate through it. He loves you but He is not going to follow you around and force you to serve Him. Do not allow the devil to make you go through so much pain that you won't have a choice but to run to God. He is a Dad that knows what's best for you because he made you a certain way.

 My parents told us a story when we were little about a boy who loved to play with sticks as a kid. Whenever they tried taking the stick away from him, he would cry uncontrollably. It was so bad that they would give him the stick back. Well, one day he stuck his left eye with a stick and bruised his eyeball so bad that he became blind in his left eye. As he became older, he went to his parents wanting to know what happened to his left eye. After they told him the story, he got so upset that he picked up a stick and threatened to strike his parents in their eyes. When they told him, he wouldn't stop crying. He screamed at them and said, "You should have let me cry! Why didn't you let me cry? Now I'm blind in one eye because of you." He was right, they should have done something else instead of letting him play with sticks. A good parent won't allow a child to play with a dangerous object and won't care if the child cries when they take the object from the child. We found that story to be funny as kids, and we could not stop laughing about it. This happens a lot with our prayers. We often pray about things that are not good for us at the time. I can just see God looking at it and saying, NO, I'm not giving that to her. She will kill herself if I did. When we pray and we don't receive the answer, we have to trust that God knows best.

How To Stay Out of Jail-God's Way

CHAPTER 3: THE BIBLE

The Bible is a practice workbook for supernatural experiences. Supernatural simply means "connecting to the spiritual world." It first lays out the foundation on how it works using men of old as examples. The more you learn and practice the better you become. It is not literature. As you grow, you learn which parts of the Bible relate to your journey and destiny. Then, you concentrate on those characters for optimum results. If you stay at it, you will master it to perfection. However, to become great at it, you have to make it a way of life. Daily practice will help you to make it into a lifestyle. Then, the benefits begin to come and you will know for sure that heaven has qualified you. Yes, sir, you have to qualify to have certain things in the realm of power. Things are not just given to you; you have to prove that you are capable of handling the power of God. In my life, when I read the Bible, I can feel demonic objects lose their grip as I read. I know this doesn't happen to everyone but it has that type of effect on my body. I usually read a minimum of 5 chapters daily. So I know there is tremendous power in the Word of God. You slowly read with a purpose, and you read daily. As you do, you are engaging with the supernatural world and attracting the spirit of prayer. The prayer dimension is a place where solutions are derived, and where dialogue takes place to resolve a matter. It is the same thing for prayer. When you start praying for hours and you continue to pray for days. You start knocking on the door of solutions. That dimension of God will show up after a while, and the effects of it will cause spirits to find out who is doing that. If you continue, they will find a way to distract you so you can stop.

They will create a situation at home or at work. All of a sudden your best friend needs your help. Your mum is not feeling good. My favorite is when you start fighting with your wife over the smallest stuff. It is all set up to cause you to stop praying like that. Pay attention and remain calm but wise. Your prayer is applying pressure in the spirit realm. That pressure will limit demons, that pressure will cause angels to engage demons in a fight. They don't want that because God always wins. Reading the Bible will add power to your life that you sometimes didn't know you had. You will find yourself praying for sick people and they get better. When you engage the principles in the Bible something happens in the spirit realm. The Bible is a book that tells you what to do to be effective. It is not just in this world, but it is in the supernatural world where spirits exist just like here. If you are ignorant of the supernatural as most people are, you will find yourself frustrated with this life because you have not learned to get assistance from God. I have seen people pray for their loved ones and friends out of prison.

With God, all things are possible, and time has no limitation. He can use speed to make up for lost time if He chooses to do it. God can bless you in a way that makes up for lost time in your life. Your 10-15years of frustrations and disappointments can be made up in a year. He can give you a blessing that will overcome every problem you've ever had. Please remember that a lot of people have left the faith because in their mind, God didn't show up on time. In this generation, the devil has come up with different schemes to deceive the younger generation. You hear people saying Jesus was just a man, the Bible is not real, the church wants to control you, and preachers are thieves only looking for your money, etc. This is a deception from the devil. If he can conceal the truth and cause you to believe a lie he will succeed in robbing you of your rights as a believer. When you start believing his lies, you disconnect from the church. I have heard all types of stories. There are people who have been molested and treated badly in the church. Some of it is true, but a believer in Christ Jesus cannot stop going to church. The enemy will change your mindset the longer you stay away from the House of God. Do you know that God comes to church often to help His children with different problems? This often happens more in church than any other place without people knowing he came. He is constantly helping; you just don't know it. A church is wherever believers or the saints are gathered. However, you are sitting at home. To stay away from church is to miss out on God's visitation regularly. You will start believing that darkness is light and light is darkness. The devil will start visiting you at home, while people in church are receiving blessings from God. It is a trick of the enemy. If you don't like a particular church, find another one. Still, the idea that you don't need church is like saying you don't need God. No pastor, preacher, evangelist, or teacher can control what God chooses to do on any given day in a church service. He is preaching the gospel and God is doing work that he doesn't have any idea about. It is not always about him or her. The church is a building that is capable of hosting the presence of God. If you stay away from such a place where would you experience such a grace, such anointing, and power of God? I know this book is about how to stay out of Jail but I thought I would lay some foundations of truth to help you achieve your goal of staying out of jail God's way.

CHAPTER 4: HELP ME STAY OUT OF JAIL

You can stay out of jail if you learn how to do a few things. This is not possible without God's help. Here are some of the things you should practice:

1. Know God for yourself
2. Control your Anger
3. Life is not about being the best
4. Humble yourself- Humility is like Magic
5. God's time – there is a time called God's time for you to receive a particular blessing.
6. Refuse to be offended – (This is the hardest to do. This is also my favorite)
7. Practice Honesty and Integrity.

KNOW GOD FOR YOURSELF

The idea of church is to introduce you to the Father and our Lord Jesus Christ. We introduce you to Christ so you can engage Him yourself. Just because you can engage Him on your own at home is not a reason to say you don't need to go to church. Corporate anointing cannot be received by yourself at home. To know God for yourself, you have to learn how to read and study the Bible daily, praise and worship God, and learn how to pray with all seriousness. In doing this you will learn how to engage the Spirit of God faster. You can invite Him and He will come. Everyone has a particular way to engage the Spirit of God. You have to learn your way of inviting God the Spirit. You will know once you keep practicing how to do it, and which aspect of God works for you. It could be praise, worship, dancing, playing the guitar, etc. For me, it is in prayer and worship that

I engage the Spirit of God to come. Please understand when you are serving God that you are not the boss. You are a servant meaning He will not come whenever you want Him to come. He can show up in two minutes, or it could take Him six months to show up. Sometimes you have to prove that you are serious before He comes. It might take a while but the key is to keep doing it until He shows up. Jacob said "I will not let You go unless You bless me." Sometimes that is what it takes. When you know God for yourself, you will know what worked the last time. You will keep repeating the same routine to invite His presence. Dancing before the lord is powerful. In 2 Samuel 6:14, David danced before the Lord with all his might, while wearing a priestly garment. So David and all the people of Israel brought up the Ark of the Lord with Shouts of Joy and the blowing of ram's horns.

You can use dancing and shouting unto the Lord to disarm and disengage the enemy. This is a spiritual strategy. The reason we need to know God is because we need God to defeat the enemy. Don't be fooled. No human can win a war with the devil without God. It doesn't matter how spiritual you are. This is true even if you are a pastor, prophet, or preacher, etc. You are who you are by the grace of God. It is that grace that will help you to not rely on your own power or strength. People think if you are rich on the earth that it means you are successful. That's very funny because I know for sure the devil can give you money in exchange for your soul. Mark 8:36 (KJV) says, "For what shall it profit a man, if he shall gain the whole world and lose his own soul?" I don't want to be rich and go to hell. I want the success that God gives. I want favor where God can bless me without qualification. Also, I will still be a special guest in heaven for doing God's will on the earth. That's how David and Solomon did it, and they were just men like us. We can achieve the same. As I write and read back what I'm writing, I am amazed as to what is written. It is unbelievable to understand the knowledge of God. I want you to know for sure as you navigate your way into the things of God. You can be praying, speaking in tongues, praising Him, worshipping Him, dancing, reading, studying the word, etc. You will start to see the ones you enjoy. Pay attention to this. It is your key to the supernatural. Every individual who is a believer has to learn how to invite His presence. What you love whether its worship, praises, etc., will help you get there faster. I'm teaching you the deep things of God. These are the things that if you don't learn it your life as a believer will be filled with frustration and disgust. It will be as if the whole experience is fake. Once in a while I get a chance to speak into someone's life by the Spirit and people are amazed as to the world of knowledge. "How did you know that?" They will ask and I will tell them there is a God in the heavens, highly exalted above men, above money, above all things. He can reveal secrets. Get to know Him, and your life will never be the same. You can have heaven on earth. Satan is deceiving us today. People think that their life is a failure if they didn't become rich. Wow, what a lie!

Everyone is not here for success. Believe it or not, some people are not here to live long. It means some will die early. We are using money and riches as a measuring stick for success. Success is accomplishing your God-given assignment on the earth. You have to get this understanding because you can be successful in the earth with riches and prosperity but a failure in your God-given assignment to you. Do you know why God made you? Are you here to help orphans? Are you here to give hope to the hopeless? Maybe you are here to give out free Bibles and encourage people. Or, like most people, you have given yourself a plan of your own. Heaven will not assist you in carrying out your plan. God is obligated to help you carry out His plan if you consult with Him. Most people will consult God when they are stuck. The Bible says there was a generation that did not know the ways of their father. A generation that didn't know God. They abandoned their assignments and were carried away with their desires. It means God was not in it. They were doing whatsoever they wanted and they justified it with their reason. This is dangerous. That is how the earth was destroyed in the past. You are created to fulfill a need in this generation or to solve a problem. You can do something special, and it will be something no one else can do like you can do. It will take you, being committed to solve that problem. To fix it according to God's time, we need you to take your rightful place in God. It might take us five years to solve a one-year problem because you didn't take your rightful place. We need you.

CHAPTER 5: CONTROL YOUR ANGER

Those who seem to have gotten ahead in their Christian walk are those who learned and came to a realization that they needed God in every aspect of their life. Do you know this for sure? Let me explain how you can know if you've come to the truth that you need God. A person who knows they need God with everything will hardly make decisions without consulting Him. It will be the important stuff, and not asking Him if you should brush your teeth. Some examples would be if I wanted to leave a job or if I wanted to go to a particular place for vacation. What approach would I take in engaging my kids with different issues? It shows you realize God is greater than you. To succeed in everything this book is talking about, you need to turn to God to give you strength. If not, when you attempt to do these things, the enemy will fight you and you will quit without realizing that this process will work for you. If God has somehow touched your heart to get this book, then He wants to use it to help you. There are many other ways God could have used in helping you but he chose this path for you. You need to know you won't succeed if He isn't helping you. Anger is spiritual, meaning it is a spirit and you cannot defeat a spirit on any level with common sense. They are defeated with spiritual insight. It means that God knows that particular spirit and He will reveal to you how to defeat him or her. There is a knowing behind the scenes beyond human understanding. That insight can only come from God. No man can give you that insight. Anytime I'm coaching people on anger, I always tell them to start by refusing to be upset about anything. It doesn't matter what, they can learn later on as to how to make adjustments to their feelings. It is your refusal to be offended that will ground you to a place of not losing control. The agitator behind the scenes will start getting frustrated. When their evil tricks won't work anymore they will leave you and start looking for another way to come back to you. These are life mysteries. Behind the scenes, light and darkness is fighting over the control of a human mind. You can get involved by laying out a way to decide for them. You can choose light or God by your behavior, and not your speech. The church is filled with people who talk like they are saved, but their lives show something completely different. Why do you think your life becomes more difficult when you get serious with God? It is because that is when you become a threat. The devil is not worried about you while you were pretending. You can't pretend in the spirit; you can pretend to other human beings. Every spirit sees you for exactly what you are. They know who you are, and not for whom you pretend to be. All power belongs to God even if you are not aware of it. God is the source of power to succeed in life, the devil is the source of wickedness in life. He comes to steal, kill and destroy (John 10:10). His greatest tools today are deception and money. Human beings are crazy about money, but they are mostly for the wrong reasons. Ask the average person why they want to be rich. They will start naming the things they want to buy. So the devil has set a system for people to chase money all their life without paying attention to their soul. Even if you end up getting money, you end up losing your soul in the process. Money is not evil, but you are supposed to have a healthy soul while making money. A soul that serves God's agenda is the key, and not your own agenda. The devil is really after your soul, and will give you money in exchange for your soul. He is a great manipulator. I'm not praising him but I know him. I'm a man of encounter, for both good and bad reasons. In my spiritual journey, I have experienced demons and angels somewhat regularly. I speak from experience. It is not something that I have read.

Your constant dialogue with God in prayer will give you the power to overcome anger and anything else in life.

I have learned not to allow the workings of life to define where I'm in life. This is what I mean, just because I currently don't have a lot of money does not mean I'm not right with God. Money is good, but if you don't learn to be happy when things are not good, you won't be happy when money comes. You will always want more money. "Though he slay me, yet will I trust in Him: but I will maintain mine own ways before Him." Job 13:15 (KJV) There is a power of God fighting the darkness in your life as you read this book. God is amazing, but you have to engage Him to find out. I was telling my daughter two weeks ago that the secret to life is your ability as a Christian to engage God. A man who doesn't engage God in prayer is hopeless. When you talk to God in prayer, He will make difficult situations in your life look so easy. He will fix your life in a way that His peace that surpasses all understanding will come all over you.

CHAPTER 6: LIFE IS NOT ABOUT BEING THE BEST

The best in what? That is a joke. It is a deception by the enemy. Now you should aspire to get the most out of your life in God according to His will. In this kingdom, it is not a competition to be the best. It is about accomplishing the will of God. We don't compete with each other because our assignments are different. No two people have the same assignment. Some people will be sent to help you in accomplishing your assignment. The battle is over who gets to control your life without your awareness. I'm letting you know so that you would be aware of the 'behind the scenes' dealings. If you are in jail, it is either the devil put you there or in some cases God allowed it to keep you alive or to fulfill an assignment. How would you know? You have to talk to Him to find out.

The devil wants to use you to initiate evil activities in this world, and God wants to use you to initiate good in the earth. There is no neutral ground. You are either doing God's work or the devil's work. No man is strong enough to avoid both. These spirits are over 2,000 years old. They have studied human behavior longer than you have been alive. Over time they have mastered life in more ways than you can imagine. They have studied your family lineage and your family tendencies. They know what your father used to do. They know the patterns of your family. They use techniques which worked on your dad, and your mum, so they can access you the same way. The demons who killed your father would share information on how they succeeded with the demons working on you. They know you were molested, abused or raped so they begin to use it against you. It becomes a weak point. The enemy has a very sophisticated system. It is not random. Some people don't seem to have any problems. The devil has already got most of these people so he doesn't have to fight them. Those same people will flaunt their money and show off. It is a joke because many have sold their soul to the enemy. He has absolute control over them, and he is telling them what to do. Your engagement in prayer is your cheat sheet. God will sometimes say to not go into work today. Stay home and pray. What you don't know is that an accident has been set for you that day. If you listen and humble yourself, you will avoid it. If you don't, the grace of God might only be able to save you from dying, but you end up in the hospital, or in a wheelchair. It could all have been avoided if you listened. Engaging God in prayer is everything to a believer. A lot of people go to prophets or psychics, etc. Psychics are evil. Never go to a psychic. A psychic will open an evil portal in your life. A portal is a door, which is a channel of evil. It is a password to your life in the spirit. You don't want that.

Become a friend of God. David was a friend of God. A friend of God is someone who has an interest in the dealings of God. I don't want to see my friends suffer, I will extend myself to help them if they need my help. With the right motive, a friend of God can achieve a lot with heaven. There was a time and season in my life that God showed me pictures of people and what to pray for about them. I prayed for people I had never met and people I didn't know. I remember a missionary from Asia. God showed me this man, and said he was in one of the Arab countries. He has been praying to be released from jail, but that he will be beheaded in the next few days. He asked me to pray that His grace is sufficient for him and that he finds peace. I never met him, but I will probably see him in heaven. I stated at the beginning of this book that there are people who came to the earth for a short time. Everyone is not here to stay long. That was his fate, and a lot of the apostles died the same way. There are activities of heaven every day taking place that is not on television. Men and women are working for God and the agenda of heaven without anyone patting them on their backs. In one of my encounters, He told me to offer a certain prayer because heaven needed it to act on the earth. I had this one experience where demons were traveling to India, and the Spirit said to bind and hinder them. I started praying and binding the devil. It usually keeps them stuck in the atmosphere for three days. It distorts their efforts and slows down their mission allowing angels to engage them. It also limits their damage to the area. When you become a friend of God, He will share a need in heaven and you can play a part to accomplish things on the earth. I have had enough evil in my life to question God. However, I love Him and I can't help it. Sometimes I pray this prayer, "Father, what do you need me to do in the earth today?". There are times when He will tell me, and there are times he will be quiet. There are times when I'm not supposed to know so He won't say anything. I don't get upset. He is my God. I try as much as I can to not get offended with Him. Everything He does is for your benefit. His silence is for a reason, and I trust Him. Romans 8:28 (KJV) "And we know that all things work together for good to them that love God, to them who are called according to his purpose."

I just felt like saying this prayer right now. "Father God I bless Your name for this day. Thank you for dealing with my stubbornness, carelessness, and foolishness. I humble myself before You today as You continue to prune me. Refine me into what You want me to be. Help me to please You as I write these words down. Let Your power move in Your people as they read these words. Let them experience an encounter with You as they read. Reveal Yourself and make Yourself known to them in a mighty way. I give you praise for there is none like you. In Jesus name, Amen".

How To Stay Out of Jail-God's Way

CHAPTER 7: HUMBLE YOURSELF

Are you humble? Are there things you think are beneath you? Your level of humbleness will often show your Spiritual maturity. Also, your prayer life is a measurement of your Spiritual growth. Are you too big to fall in a church service? Or to roll on the floor by the Spirit? I'm not talking about acting it out. I'm talking about having an experience. If you are too proud, you will never experience certain aspects of God. If you are not humble, you can learn how to be humble. These are things that disarm demons. Before I started this page I felt demons come into the house. I can smell them so I knew they were here. I started commanding them to leave, and then the angels came and I knew this book was special. They are worried about it. They wanted to interfere with the writing. They do the same to everyone. The difference is that I can tell when they come around me, and I command them to leave. Find some selfless act and practice humbleness. Serve in the church. Become an usher in your church, or volunteer to help feed the homeless. Trust me, you will hate doing it in the beginning, but you are on a mission. You are practicing a good thing that you will want to become a part of your life. This is a habit you will want to adopt. Find someone who needs a ride and pick them up. Or, drop them off on your way home. When they offer you gas money, you can refuse to accept the money. If they insist you tell them that God will give you a greater blessing. I had a business selling art, and a young lady with one arm came in one day looking for a job. She was so great in her presentation that I wanted to hire her, but I couldn't afford to. Many years later, I saw her at a gas station begging for money. She didn't recognize me. She told me her lights will get cut off if it's not paid that day. As she was making her case, I kept looking at her, and thinking in my head, "What has happened to you?" She was working at a parts store and she had her uniform on while she begged for money to pay her light bill. When she finished talking I said to her, "You don't remember me, do you?" She started thinking about it. "Where do I know this man from?" She thought my face looked familiar, but couldn't place where she knew me from. Then it hit her and she said, "Are you the guy who owns the art gallery at the mall." And I said, "Yes, you remembered. What happened to you? This is not the way I remember you. You were so smart and brilliant that I felt badly about not hiring you." She started to tell me that she had a baby and had some really bad experiences with the baby's father and became homeless at one point. She quickly came to herself and said, "I'm sorry, but I need to keep talking to people so I can get help for my light bill." I said to her, "I will pay the light bill. Just go ahead and finish telling me the story. When she finished the story, we went inside the gas station which also doubled for a check cashing place. I paid the light bill for her. She had such a genuine heart. She started telling me she will get paid on Thursday and that she will surely pay me back. She wanted my phone number so she could call me and arrange how to meet to give me the money back. I told her I didn't need the money back. She looked at me and said, "What type of man gives a woman money without wanting something in return? Like not sex and not the money back?". I said to her, "The kind of man who knew that his reward will be greater than you giving him the money back." I told her I will give her my number just to know how she is doing but nothing else. And I said, "God willing, we will meet again. Learn to help people out of the goodness of your heart. But do it safely. In today's society, you could pick up a stranger asking for a ride, and he turns out to be a killer. Find organizations that do it for a living and help them do it. There are many non-profit organizations everywhere doing charity work. When you see an old lady carrying something heavy, stop and help her. Sometimes you will meet angels and buy favor like you have never seen in your life. You will never be good at anything you don't practice. Practice makes perfect.

How To Stay Out of Jail-God's Way

CHAPTER 8: GOD'S TIME

There is a time for everything under the sun. A time to be born and a time to die. (Ecclesiastes 3:8). When you learn who God is, you learn to trust Him. You stay patient knowing that He who started a good work in you will perform it until the day of Christ Jesus (Philippians 1:6). To trust God is to know He has not forgotten about you. He is still on the throne. It is a great throne, and it is like no other. God's timing will happen when He is ready to bless you. It will happen when you've completed your assignment, and when you have passed with flying colors. You didn't curse God when it was bad. When the set time has come, God will show why He is God. Many things happening in your life now are part of your training. Pay attention and don't quit because it has become difficult. Trust God and wait on Him. I will share a little bit of my life story with you. I was 17 years old, in high school, and living in Nigeria. It was then when I first heard God call my name. It was about 5 pm, and I was walking to the soccer field to play. I heard someone call my name. I turned around to see who called me, but I didn't see anyone. I kept going, and I heard my name again. I turned around for the second time and I didn't see anyone. Then it hit me, my father the late Chief Samuel Akwari Okoronkwo would tell us stories of the Bible every day before he prayed for us. He would pray so long we would all fall asleep. Boy, did he get upset that we were sleeping! We were just kids and didn't want to be there. So I heard my name the third time and I remembered the story of Samuel. He responded by saying, "Speak Lord, for your servant is listening." Once I said it, He started speaking. He said, "I'm the God of your father, the One he's praying to every day." And He said, "I want you to do something for Me." and I said, "why?" He said, "When I ask you to do something, you need to do it first before you ask me questions." He said, "Look straight ahead, and you see the building right in front of you. I want you to speak in tongues and walk around it three times. I was already speaking in tongues at the time so I did it. When I got back to where I started He said, "I want you to hold prayers in this building every day at 4.30 pm." I gathered my friends together. Although, I had to beg for some of them to come. When we got there, He said to have them form a circle, and then open a door to walk into the circle while everyone was praying. He had me stand back about six feet to the circle, then speak in tongues and walk into the circle. When I did, everyone fell to the floor. Wow. That was my first encounter with God, and my life has never been the same. It was such a fall that I thought some had gotten hurt, but everyone got up and were fine without any pain. Welcome to my life experience with God! Things have been happening ever since. I hosted a program in high school with my friends. I was convinced the blind would see and the lame would walk. Well, the program took place and nothing happened. This was in the 12th grade. I was so disappointed that I walked away from God and Ministry. I went far away to college just to get away. I didn't want to influence any of the young ones that looked up to me to backslide. I didn't share my frustrations with them. I held it inside, as I was the person everyone looked up to. After high school, I handed over my position as President of the Christian group called Scripture union to a Junior Student to succeed me and I left. I remember that they were having problems at some point, and they came to my home for help. Because everyone held me in such high regards, they wanted me to come and talk to the other students. Some of the members were being rebellious. I was still upset and confused about the revival, so I didn't go. I told them I will pray for the power of God to come upon them to enable them to carry out the task. I prayed for them, and the power of God came upon them. They were slain in the spirit right in my bedroom. They stayed on the floor for a while, and then they got up. I told them everything would be fine. They left and went back to school. Still, I was so upset that I didn't go back to church. I was confused. I said to myself, "If God didn't do it and I felt He would, how could I ever trust Him?" I was just 18 years at the time. I walked away from ministry and everything about it. I started doing everything I was big and bad enough to do. I started smoking and doing all types of stuff. The devil was trying to kill me. I would travel to the United States 4 years later. It took another 3 years for me to return to the things of God. I was going to college and I had a security job while in school. One day I was standing outside a building when a man walked past me, he gave me a flyer and it read "Smile Jesus loves you". It made me upset. I had gotten married, and I told my wife my story. The man who gave me the flyer came back to talk to me. He said the Spirit of God said to go back and talk to him. He started to prophesy to me. The more he spoke the more upset I got. I didn't say a word and he said to me, "Do you understand what I'm saying to you?" This is the prophecy he gave me in a quote.

"The Lord said to tell you it is time to come back to Him. I have plans for your life and you know too much to stay away from Me. I have allowed you to do what you wanted to do but now it is time to come back to Me".

I looked at him like you have no idea what happened to me. I was embarrassed by God. I'm thinking this all in my head. He started prophesying again in quote

"I will make things clearer to you. Just come back. It's time." He looked at me and said, "The Lord is telling me I don't need to explain things to you. That you have a very high level of understanding. That you are not as ordinary as you look". That was it, and he started to walk away from me. I went home and told my wife of my experience. "You wouldn't believe what happened to me today." I told her the story and she said, "It might be time to go back. She said to me, "Look, I'm American but I have never heard anyone preach and teach the gospel the way you do. You truly have a gift; you should consider going back to God." I listened and started making my way back to the church. Ladies and

Gentlemen, I have made mistakes even after I came back. I'm not your perfect man of God. But I'm a man full of mysteries, with encounters like you can't imagine. This is my journey. The Lord explained to me that He is the one in charge. He said everything that He gives is within His will and plan. I have to learn to seek Him for His will. I don't need to do things my way and expect Him to show up. I have to get authorization before I start doing things. Just because He used me to perform one miracle doesn't mean I can decide what He will do next. I'm not in charge, but He is. Once I gained that understanding, I realized why the miracles didn't happen. I remember saying to Him that I had faith, and He said, "Faith operates within My will. You cannot go doing whatever you want and expect faith to help you achieve it. When you start doing what you want, you start hindering and interfering with other things I'm doing."

CHAPTER 9: REFUSE TO BE OFFENDED

This is my favorite. For many years, I was struggling with anger. As a man from African decent, specifically Nigeria, anger was a regular practice back home. If you wanted to be taken seriously, you made your point emphatically, and used hand gestures. It is an attempt to show that you not kidding and that there will be consequences. So when you meet an African speaking with force, you now understand why he is doing that. We come from a place where you have to be forceful to be taken seriously. The laws of the land are not enforced. If you have money, you have the upper hand. However, that is a topic for another day. I was dealing with anger in my life. It started destroying things in my life, and the relationships all around me. Anger is a spirit. I began to pray and ask God for strength to overcome anger. One day it hit me like a download from heaven. Refuse to be offended. It means that no matter what happens to you and around you, you do not express any form of anger. This is because you have not been able to filter through your emotions to know what you should be upset about and what you should not be upset about.

As I started doing this, I was able to see clearly. I made adjustments by determining what I should be upset or irritated about. If I have a brother, I should know my brother if we grew up together. With my brother, I'm aware of what he can be trusted with and what not to expect from him. What happens if I kept trusting him with responsibilities he couldn't handle, and then I ignore his track record? The outcome is on me. This is not judgment, but this is saying, 'Show me that you are capable of doing this and I will trust you again, and count on you to get it done. It is about your actions, not your words.' I saw a transformation in my life as I did this. I didn't get upset as often as I used to. I figured out what was important, and which parts of my life needed attention. I realized what I should be working on at each stage of my life. It changed my life. One Word from the Lord can change everything about you. My friends started noticing that I seemed happier, and it was amazing. After a while, I was so excited that I started teaching my friends how to do it. I begin to see their lives change because they refused to be offended. This is something you practice for a season. You can practice it for at least four months out of the year, and it works. Demonic spirits are initiating the affairs of your life, and they are more dominant when you are not serving God. Without God, you have nothing to fight them off with. There is no light. When you do serve God, they watch to see how much you know about God. Knowing God is just the beginning. You have to learn how to do things to ensure that demons cannot have control over your life. If you are ignorant, they will manipulate your life, even as a believer in Christ Jesus.

Christianity is not for lazy people. They have devices that attach to your body to help control you with a remote from their kingdom. They can channel thoughts into your head. We call that demonic wiring. You think you are in charge but you are not. You hear people say something told me to shoot them. They feed you ideas through voices or just something that came to you. The more they attach to you; the more they control you.

Reading the Bible and hearing the Bible are some of the tools you can use to detach or disconnect what is attached to you. Worshipping and singing praises of gospel music can also help as you learn how to use these tools. Praising and worshipping God invites angels to come. Certain angels will come, and their presence will remove the devices from your body. When you constantly are in the presence of God, you have a much better chance to be whole. 2 Timothy 1:7 (NKJV) says, "For God has not given us a spirit of fear but of power and of love and of a sound mind." I'm not trying to scare you. However, these are things God has allowed me to see, and He wants me to share it with you. The more you don't read, pray and worship or praise God, the more you become less like Him. Without these evil devices, men would easily hear God, and communicate and dialogue with Him regularly. These instruments are used to establish a connection to the devil instead of God. There is a war over who gets access to your body. It is a war between good and evil. Demons and angels are fighting over your body. That is how important you are! These devices come as a liquid, and most times they will come while you are sleeping. It can be food in your sleep, passing things through your anus into your body. Your anus is a door. Disgusting? Yes, I agree, but they don't care. Many go to sleep, and wake up with a headache, back pain, etc. These are symptoms where an encounter took place while you were sleeping. Don't be afraid. When you experience these things, pray immediately, and command it out of your body. When they see that you know what to do, they will stop doing it and change their strategy. Mental illness today is largely credited to demons invisible to humans. Most of these people can see spirits, but we classify them as crazy instead of gifted. Most people with mental illnesses are very gifted people who don't know what to do with what they see, because regular people tell them they are crazy. They just need to know how to control what they see and they will be as normal as you and I. The things I see and encounter will drive the normal person crazy, but it is a normal life for me because you will never know unless I told you. Things like praying, fasting, reading the Bible, praising God and worshipping Him are things that create pressure in the atmosphere and cause spirits to change course. When I feel the presence of demons in my home, I don't always have to pray. I can just play gospel music, and it will irritate the evil spirit. Then, the spirit would leave. There are other times when I will have to worship with intensity for the spirit to leave. As you use these tools, you will know which one works for you. It is not random because every individual is designed to use a particular tool. How do you know which tool to use? By practicing, start reading the Bible, praising and worshiping God.

Speaking in tongues, and pay attention to what happens while you are doing it. You have to put some time into this. This is an investment into your destiny. Trust me, you need it. Maybe an hour or more. There is going to be an encounter if you don't quit. Do not be afraid, keep going. When it happens, what where you practicing? Were you praying, singing or speaking in tongues? Whatever you were doing when it happened is your access tool. Do not forget that. It is this tool that will help you get in the presence of God faster. Your personal password. Everybody's password is different. Start using your password by repeating what you did. This is how you can reach the Spirit of God. By using your own personal access tool which is your password.

These gospel tools, along with hearing God's voice, if you are lucky, will change your life for good. Church participation is vital in your walk with God. When the presence of God comes, it makes everything new. It rejuvenates the human body and will help in removing evil devices of the enemy. Life is deep and very spiritual. Spiritual refers to what you don't see. Believe it or not, what you don't see control what you see. What you don't see triggers and initiates what you see.

CHAPTER 10: PRACTICE HONESTY & INTEGRITY

You have to practice honesty and integrity to be good at it. Most things in life are learned behavior. Practicing good behavior with God's help. This example will help to change you into a better version of yourself. You can practice the presence of God meaning you can practice how to invite the Spirit of God. It will help you learn how you activate and trigger God's presence to come. Anyone can learn how to do it. In the earlier chapters, I talked about how you can use a particular aspect of God's activity that you enjoy the most to call His presence. It could be praising, worshipping, reading the Bible, or dancing in the Lord. You can choose whichever aspect that you enjoy. This is because what you enjoy will engage your soul, your spirit and your mind at the same time. You can lose yourself completely, and that's when He comes. It takes all of you. The reason why people don't experience God is that they lack a sense of sincerity. You are praying, but you are worried about your bills at the same time. You will never connect to God in that way. He needs all of you, especially the sincerity of your heart. There is a part of you that needs to acknowledge that you came to the source of life. It is a place of total submission.

      Choose to be honest, as it really pays off. As a believer, we are supposed to always tell the truth. It is when you have practiced how to tell the truth, and you believe that there are benefits to it. This is when it will work in your life. It will make your life free of stress because you don't have to keep up with lies. You are building habits that will help you later in life. These are habits that you can pass on to your children. Integrity is defined as the quality of being honest and having a strong moral principle; moral uprightness. These are some of the ways in which you can incorporate honesty and integrity:

1) Pay attention to your environment
2) Take responsibility
3) Keep your word
4) Stay focused.

Sex is a covenant where you become one with another person. You exchange deep virtues and treasures inside of you with the other person. An evil spirit can steal a gift from you during sex. You tie your soul with that individual. When your soul is tied to another person, that individual will now have access to you. This individual spiritually becomes a husband or a wife and will begin to have rights that a wife or husband would have. The evil spirit begins to use these rights to do evil in your life. It can cancel out good things coming to you, it can fight your real wife or husband. In some cases, it can kill that individual.

It is a serious problem. Every spiritual content in that individual comes inside of you. Evil and good can both come inside. If you notice after having sex with a person, you may start having experiences that you didn't have before. So often evil spirits will appear as human beings of the opposite sex to entice you and sleep with you. This will help them in controlling you from their kingdom. During the sexual exchange, a device goes inside of you. Through that device, that same spirit will start appearing at night to sleep with you either physically or in your sleep. In my experience, it may appear every time something good is about to happen to you. That spirit appears, sleeps with you and disconnects the good thing coming. These evil spirits will often be able to see the good thing coming before you do.

For your part, your constant engagement with the things of God keeps them away.

If you don't know this, everybody you see is not human. Some have had sex with demons who present themselves as humans just like angels often show up as human beings. Please be careful about sleeping with different people. It is dangerous. Very often, night clubs are filled with demons or prostitutes on the roadside etc. I have seen people lose their life because they could not control the consequences as a result of sleeping with a demon. This is why the Bible teaches that you get married before having sex. Many of us, including me, have had sex with different partners, but it is wrong. This experience I just explained happened to me. We have to train ourselves to obey the Word of God. It is never easy but we can all try our best. That is all that God requires of us. We need to give our best.

CHAPTER 11: IF YOU ARE IN JAIL

There are two types of jail. They are spiritual and physical. If you are in a spiritual jail, you will find yourself running around in circles. It is like you are stuck in the same place for many years. This is because you are not growing spiritually. There is nothing new in your spiritual walk. You have to keep growing and adding to what you know already. One of the many ways you can do this is by reading and studying to add to your knowledge. Whatever new thing you add will help your life to grow. You have to make sure you are adding the right information. Studying the Word of God will help to increase your Spiritual growth. The Word brings light and that light is illumination. Illumination is when the light comes on, and you get understanding. Things are made very clear to you. If you find yourself locked up in jail, you should embark on a Spiritual journey to secure your release. Mass incarceration is quite horrible. Humans are playing God and people are treated like animals. Men are passing judgment and condemning God's creation. This is a dilemma. I'm not saying that people should not pay for what they have done, but we are making a business out of it instead of investing in rehabilitating these people back into society. Wherever you find yourself in jail, I want you to know that God is aware of your situation and where you are. There are often life lessons you need to learn while you are sitting in jail. If you don't learn it and you get released, you will find yourself back in jail again. If you are a repeat offender, you can't help yourself. You are always going in and out of jail. You are missing something. You are missing the relationship with God. God has a way of getting a man's attention. You can do it the easy way or the hard way.

Richard Okoronkwo

  I believe that mass incarceration relates to the fact that fathers are not at home. This is a demonic strategy. Take the man out of any family and you have a chance to destroy the whole family. It is a strategy to destroy more than one person at a time because it affects the whole family. Men and women who had no one to show them what to do and how to behave usually end up in jail. Without mentors, such as parents or guardians, life can be quite difficult. So the first strategy of fixing this is to find mentors, teachers, and guardians. If you grew up without a father, you need a father. Find a father figure. If you grew up without a mother, find a mother figure. You will continue to have that void until you fix it. Please understand that getting an education will not fix the fact that you need a father or mother in your life. You are glossing over issues without fixing them. Learn to fix issues in your life and don't ignore it. If you were sexually molested, go talk to someone, and get help. If you don't, all the men and women in your life will suffer the consequences, and it will affect your kids. It is important to identify what is lacking in your life. Everyone is lacking something. I don't care who you are. There must be something you should be working on to make yourself more like Jesus Christ. Jesus Christ is the standard. Over time, people will usually criticize you about what is missing in your life, your ability, and your hygiene. Whatever it is, people will usually point it out. Get some help.

    As I'm writing this, I need help in my life and I'm getting the help I need. When help arrives and you figure it out, you will start growing. You now know how to handle something that plagued you for a long time. I see too many people refusing to get help. If you don't get help, you will stay stuck. You will keep making the same mistakes for the rest of your life. Every year, you should add a quality you didn't have before every year. Most people want to make money. So they chase money and forget knowledge. When you look back, you lack money and knowledge.

Sounding professional doesn't make you smart. It might get you in the door, but without substance, you can't stay there. Pretending to be something you are not might get you in the door. Eventually, your true colors will show. A woman who works hard to look good on the outside would attract a man. Yet, you won't be able to keep him because you have no homemaking skills, you don't cook, you don't clean, and you never learned how to take care of a man. Trust me, your beauty will fade. You need more than outer beauty. A woman needs marriage skills, instead of thinking about what can her spouse do for her. This is vain. A man needs to learn how to take care of his family and his wife. He needs to learn what it means to be a husband. If you don't know, you can learn. If you don't develop the skills of how to take care of your home, kids and the woman, eventually he or she will leave you. All over this country, there are beautiful women. Yet, when you get close to them, they lack substance. They are nothing more than their face or body. We are losing the art of what it takes to be a woman. Women in the past have helped to mold the lives of many great men. Today, a lot of women lack character. They want to control the man, and want them to do whatever they want. That type of woman, no matter what she looks like, will keep switching men and will have multiple partners. She will be endangering her life. Do you have the quality to show a good man why he should stay? The fact that you are attractive is not enough. It works on social media and TV. It does not work in real life. Men and women need to work on themselves to develop skills that will make a marriage work. In a Godly home, the woman should never be in charge. This is not sexism. This is Biblical. God holds the man accountable. It is his job to lead his family. If he is not capable, the women can temporarily lead while he learns how to lead. Men should learn how to lead. It is hard for a woman to follow you when you are not capable of leading. Now back to my original concept. These are the things you should practice to get out of jail.

1)Read the Bible daily
2)Pray daily
3)Dream daily
4)You have to do it until you get results.

How To Stay Out of Jail-God's Way

CHAPTER 12: SHAME

Shame can keep you in bondage. It could be because of a lack of money, sickness, or any type of reproach. It can cause you to hide. I pray you are delivered. You can learn to embrace your failure, and use it for your testimony. I hear people saying that they pray all the time and they don't understand while all these bad things are happening to them. Stand with God, and never give up because of your trouble. Your trouble is a sign that you are making progress in the realm of the Spirit. The devil is hitting you with all he's got. He wants to stop you, but the wind of God will give you strength. Shame is a thief. Do not allow it to rob you of your blessings. Let shame fall like the walls of Jericho. Own what you have done. In regards with what happened to you, forgive yourself, and get ready for your testimony. Let the chain of affliction fall right now. I break the chain now in the name of Jesus. There is no shame in Christ Jesus. I can start off by telling you I have failed a few times. Still, God has kept me. Many of us have carried shame from something that happen to us a long time ago and we refuse to let it go. We need to forgive ourselves, and instead we blame ourselves for it. Rape victims feel they did something to contribute to why it happened to them.

Today, Jesus Christ is standing by waiting to forgive everything concerning your past.

Just ask and you will receive. As you receive it, forgive yourself and start a new chapter in your life. Whether you believe it was your fault, or you thought someone took advantage of you, you can receive salvation in Christ Jesus.

Then, you can be set free. Today, I want you to receive that freedom. Stand up right now, raise both hands in the air and speak out loud "I receive freedom from my past wrongdoing in Jesus name, Amen". Say it three times. Ladies and Gentlemen, keep saying it until you believe it. Are you aware that Jesus loves you? He loves you more than your past. "You mean in spite of everything I have done, He still loves me?" "Yes, Sir/Madam, He loves you so much that He will never give up on you. I mean that. John 3:16 (KJV) says, "For God so loved the world that he gave his only begotten Son that whosoever believeth in Him should not perish, but have everlasting life." The love of God is like a giant man carrying a little girl in his hands. He is making sure no one is going to hurt her. That's how important you are.

No more can shame keep you in bondage. You are free, and you are free in Jesus' name.

Receive your freedom from shame today in the name of Jesus, Amen. Your best is yet to come. You are not what happens to you. You are a child of the most high God. The biggest, most powerful God in creation is your Dad. Do you know this? He is bigger than everyone in creation standing together as a team. He is bigger than all the celebrities put together. He is greater than hurricanes, earthquakes and He can say a word to make it all stop. People wonder why God is allowing bad things to happen. It is because of the evil ways of men. The wickedness of men and women on earth will cause the things God created to rise up against men. In (Luke 19:39-40) says, "But some of the Pharisees in the crowd said to Him, 'Teacher, rebuke your disciples!' "I tell you," He answered, "If they remain silent, the very stones will cry out." The rocks will cry out when men refuse to praise God and take their place in God.

The question is why do you think you are in charge? You think that you can do whatever you want without consequences. Can you call the sun and the moon? Can you command the day to turn into night and the night into day? Did you set the limitation for the oceans? God did. He knows how many hairs are on your head. Learn who He is. It will help you figure life out. Creation has been in existence before you were born. You are not in charge. God is in charge. Humble yourself and learn about who He is. He is bigger than all the presidents from all the countries put together. He is a king maker. What is that thing in your past that stops you in your tracks when you remember it? It literally paralyzes you just by remembering it. The devil is using it to keep you in bondage. You have to release it. Ask God for forgiveness right now, and let it go. Release it and be set free now in the name of Jesus, Amen!

You deserve to be set free. Jesus died for you to be free. Begin now to walk into freedom. It is the type that God freely gives us. You will have no more shame. Hallelujah. We will stand in the boldness of the gospel of Jesus Christ. Let God be true and let every man be a lie. Are you one of those people who are ashamed about where you come from, including your family members, etc.? In the Kingdom of God, where you come from is not important as why you here. Your mother might be a prostitute. It doesn't matter in the Kingdom of God. What matters is discovering why God sent you here. What is it He wants you to do while you are alive? The bondage of shame is created to cause delay, and it causes you to abort your destiny. It causes you to miscarry what you are carrying, and to change course. You won't accomplish the task. The devil is not interested in you as a person, but he is interested in your assignment, which is your mission on earth. The fight is about what you are carrying on the inside of you. In order to accomplish this task, you need the help of God. The King Maker will help you to navigate through all the traps of the enemy. If God allowed you to be born and to grow up, then you are capable of any task He gave you to do only if you lean on Him. Without Him it will be impossible. You will find yourself quitting, running and confused.

How To Stay Out of Jail-God's Way

CHAPTER 13: STREET MENTALITY

I spent 8 years running a business in Decatur, Georgia. I watched how people lived a life of getting over others, which were mostly motivated by drugs and alcohol. They lived their lives on the street with no home, and no guaranteed food to eat on any given day. It becomes a survival of the fittest. Young men were dropping out of school to sell marijuana on the street. The problem is that when you are teenager (14 or younger), you tend to think that a certain amount of money is a lot of money. Young people who think $100 is a lot of money, think that a $1000 is a fortune because they are still kids.

There is a mentality permeating the street that needs to change. Men and women think that a certain lifestyle is okay, which is a lifestyle without God in it. These are some of the examples of the thought process I saw with these beloved people of God.

STREET MENTALITY

There is no food at home and the single mother doesn't have any money. Her teenage son says to himself, "I'm going to rob somebody to get money to buy food for my little brothers and sisters. He picks up a knife or a gun and goes outside looking to rob someone. It doesn't always go as planned. In some cases, he gets killed.

GOD'S WAY

Exodus 20:15(KJV) says, "Thou shalt not steal." Thinking about stealing takes away from finding a solution the right way. You need to find a permanent solution, and not a temporary one. How often would you have to steal or rob someone? This is not a solution. Quick fixes don't work. Think about people who might be able to help. Some examples would be uncles or aunties, nieces or nephews, etc. If you find someone to help, it doesn't have to stop there. How do you make sure that it doesn't happen again? Maybe the teenager can get a part time job. Explore all your options, and never consider stealing as an option. Learn to say a prayer, and God will use your mind to find the solution you need.

STREET MENTALITY

After a really bad tussle or fight, I have to prove to him or her that I'm tough. They should be afraid of me. I pick up a gun and look to shoot the individual, either openly or in secret.

GOD'S WAY

Genesis 4:10 – What have you done? Replied the Lord. "The voice of your brother's blood cries out to me from the ground. A human's blood has a voice and speaks even from the grave. Just because you killed someone and no one knew about it doesn't mean that God didn't know about it. Learn to agree and disagree without violence. It is okay to be wrong sometimes. You can learn a lot and grow that way. Losing an argument doesn't make you weak. I never met anyone who was right all the time.

STREET MENTALITY

A lady while buying gas from a convenient store leaves her purse and drives off. I opened the purse and it had $600 inside. She comes back looking for it. She asks me if I saw her purse and I say that I haven't, but I leave the area celebrating and telling people that God blessed me today.

GOD'S WAY

Genesis 20:5 thou shall not steal. Stealing is not just when you pick up a gun and point at someone. You stole that money from the lady. You have broken a God covenant that has consequences. Every crying tear from that lady will bring you pain in your life. Many wonder why their life is filled with chaos and curses. Things like stealing this lady's rent money can bring a curse on you and your children.

STREET MENTALITY

If I saw you steal something I could never say anything. If I do, I'm a snitch. You go to jail and you are looking for a way to hurt me because I spoke the truth.

GOD'S WAY

John 8:32 – they you will know the truth, and the truth will set you free. Without taking responsibility, you will continue stealing. You will either end up in jail or be killed. Take responsibility for your actions and realize that the individual who told on you didn't do anything wrong. Just because many think the same way doesn't make it right. Those who chose to go to jail instead of telling the truth will continue to do the wrong thing all their life. Change your life and stand up for what is right. It doesn't make you perfect but it is the right thing to do.

STREET MENTALITY

I have a wife, but I also have a girlfriend on the side. Almost like I have a backup plan and for others, because one woman is not enough for me.

GOD'S WAY

I Corinthians 6:18-20 Flee from sexual immorality. Every other sin a person commits is outside the body, but the sexually immoral person sins against his own body or do you not know that your body is a temple of the holy spirit within you, whom you have from God? You are not your own, for you were bought with a price. So glorify God in your body. To always take the path of doing things the wrong way will create problems in your life. If you care about pleasing God, learn to do things the right way by obeying the Bible. Stay away from disobeying God. Many today are suffering because they never cared about doing things the God way. Others think they are having fun but they are going away from the kingdom of God.

STREET MENTALITY

Sleeping with a married man or woman is very common. For a lot of people, it is not a big deal.

GOD'S WAY

I Corinthians 10:8 –we should not commit sexual immorality, as some of them did, and in one day twenty-three thousand of them died.

I have never seen anyone who kept sleeping with a married man or women that ended up in a good place. I have seen many continue to suffer because in their younger years they kept sleeping with married man or woman. Life has consequences. You should try all you can to do things the right way.

STREET MENTALITY

I'm not going to get a good job because they will cut off my food stamps.

GOD'S WAY

Acts 20:35 – in all things I have shown you that by working hard in this way we must help the weak and remember the words of the Lord Jesus, how He Himself said, and "It is more blessed to give than to receive".

We should all work hard and make sure that we are not cheating the system. Once again, attempting to stay on food stamps without trying to get a job is wrong.

STREET MENTALITY

If I tell you something you are doing wrong. I'm judging you.

GOD'S WAY

If I tell you stealing is wrong. It doesn't mean I'm judging you, it means I'm speaking truth. I Corinthians 6:2 Do ye not know that the saints shall judge the world? If the world shall be judged by you, are ye unworthy to judge the smallest matters? It is sad that you are living in sin. When you are corrected with Biblical references, you get upset.

STREET MENTALITY

If I get shot by someone, then I have to shoot them back.

GOD'S WAY

Vengeance is mine, I will repay. Roman 12:19-21 Beloved, never avenge yourselves, but leave it to the wrath of God, for it is written, Vengeance is mine, I will repay says the Lord. To the contrary, "if your enemy is hungry, feed him, if he is thirsty, give him something to drink, for by so doing you will heap burning coals on his head" Do not be overcome by evil, but overcome evil with Good.

Simply put, leave it for God. If He decides to punish a man, it will be worse than anything you can do.

While I had a business in Decatur I saw kids rob people for $10, and shoot people for $20 or less. It was quite an experience. It was one that made me appreciate growing up with a mum and dad. With time, I developed a hunger to help the young. It was not by giving them money, but by talking some sense into them. I was reasoning and explaining to them that there are good options. You are not taking your options; you are settling for the first thing that came to you which is often violence. Trying to teach these kids that they can do without violence was like telling them they are weak. No, you are not weak but you are trying to make something out of your life, to stay alive. In some cases, it was after they got in trouble a few times. That's when they realize that their strategy was not working.

    At different times, someone broke into my business. A lady came to me asking for money, and then she would tell me who did it. The same person sometimes was part of the whole scheme. Stealing and taking something that didn't belong to them was just a normal day for them. Girls as young as 14 were having sex with different people in the community for money. Grandparents would be smoking marijuana with their grandkids as young as 13. Too many senseless violence committed out of trying to prove that they are tougher than you. Gang activity also played a big part. Kids were being told that they have to shoot someone to join the gang. When you talk about God, there is a sense that God abandoned us, and allowed for us to be in this situation. Most of these people think that they have to get it together before they start going to church.

THE SOLUTION

The solution is the church, but not any type of church. What you see in these impoverished neighborhoods is a demonic spirit. A spirit that has stayed in the area for generations, and it is carrying out the same behavior and transferring the lifestyle from one generation to another. This demon can be defeated through prayer and knowledge. Prayer to break their bondage off the people and knowledge to show these individuals how to live better. The fact that everyone around you is doing the same thing creates a sense that it is normal. If you take him or her out of the area and show them a different way, their eyes will open. But the curse has to be broken. If it is not, that individual will continue to crave going back to that area. When it gets really bad, people seem to go back to what they know. I saw a church in the area providing clothing, food, shelter, haircut and assistance with bills while preaching the gospel to them. I tell you the truth, I saw these individuals doing all that without any change. They were receiving all that the church was offering without any change. These demons are stubborn. There has to be aggression with intensity to cause them to leave. Prayer with spiritual direction, and prophesy to bring understanding are both excellent. There are so many things to do. God is constantly looking for people. It is hard for God to find men and women with the right intention to execute a task for the kingdom. Many are preaching, teaching and a ministering, but their motive is wrong. God is still looking for men to obey Him and help others in the earth do His will. He will never impose His will; you have to be willing for Him to use you.

There are churches everywhere but many have lost their way. Struggle will often cause men to change course. What decision will you make when it gets really bad? This is the most common strategy the devil uses. Put a man in a really bad place financially, and then he/she will start to change their mind. Believe, it is only very few that will stay the course without changing who they are. That is the test of your Christian faith. It is easy to serve God when things are good. Take the time to develop a resolve to do God's will. Whoever said it was easy is not telling the truth. Being a Christian is not easy, but it pays off. It takes a will and God's help. Without it, it is impossible to please God.

CHAPTER 14: READ THE BIBLE DAILY

Bible reading is very important. You have to make it a habit. Consistency will take you a long way. It means that you are showing every demon and angel that you should be taken seriously. You learn to use the Word to fight your battles. I'm still trying to master this. When you engage with the Word, you are more effective. Develop a routine. Try doing it the same time every day so the spirit that is responsible for that dimension will come to visit more likely in a dream. In this case, you are inviting the Spirit of God to come visit you. Do not be afraid, as this is a good thing. I pray it happens for you in Jesus' Name Amen.

PRAY DAILY

The official line of communication between the earthly realm and the spiritual world is by prayer.

Prayer can change everything, and prayer will get you out of jail. Make no mistake about it. Are you tough enough for the type of prayers you need? Now, I will make this even better. You have to receive the Holy Ghost. Yes, speaking in tongues will elevate your communication with heaven. You have a soul, spirit, and body. Through prayer, your soul will begin to engage God on your behalf. You will be asking questions trying to find out where you are in your destiny. The soul will relate that message to your spirit, and your spirit will start adjusting to the information. Then it relates it to the body. The body is now carrying out the task. If your soul tells your spirit it's time to get him out of jail, then your spirit will send out triggers to make it happen. Angels will supernaturally carry out the task. There is a dialogue taking place between your spirit and your soul. Is he ready? Did he learn from his mistakes? Is it going to take a few more times for him to get it? If you force yourself out of jail without the learning aspect, you will find yourself back in jail. The learning creates growth. besides the fact that you have money to get out. In the spirit realm, there is no manipulation, being fake, etc. You are exactly what you are revealed to be. Your growth level is attached to you, and who you are. You will never be mistaken for what you are not. If you develop a consistent prayer life, your life will change immediately. You will start having visions and dreams about your future. I'm sharing a life-changing experience like you can never imagine. Prayer alone will bring you out of any situation. Pick a time, and pray the same time every day. Don't concentrate on the immediate result, concentrate on consistency. You want to make it a lifestyle. The mentality that if I do this for this period, my life will change is not a good one. Listen, change is coming anyways, but concentrate on developing prayer as a habit. It is in the realm of prayer that everything changes. And when your transformation arrives, you can help to change other people. This is not for a lazy person. Some of you will see angels while you are doing this. Some will have visitors from the underworld. Don't be afraid, you are becoming somebody. The secret things of life are beginning to come to you. You are moving from the realm of ordinary to extraordinary. This is the place where kings are made. Now you have to be humble. If you develop pride, it slows down your growth pattern. Pride can cost you a lot in the realm of power. Stay humble, and you will experience more growth. Prayer is everything. Heaven does not move until someone prays. I will tell you a mystery. If you develop your prayer life while in jail, you will either be in jail as an assignment from God or you are getting out. Yes, someone can go to jail for a reason. It will be as an assignment from God. Believe it. For a start, let's have a plan. This is a prayer schedule you should adopt.

BEGINNER'S PLAN

DAYS	PRAYER TIME
MONDAY	5AM -6AM
TUESDAY	5AM -6AM
WEDNESDAY	5AM -6AM
THURSDAY	5AM -6AM
FRIDAY	5AM -6AM

The idea is to pray for one hour every day.

NEXT STAGE

DAYS	PRAYER TIME
MONDAY	5AM -7AM
TUESDAY	5AM -7AM
WEDNESDAY	5AM -7AM
THURSDAY	5AM -7AM
FRIDAY	5AM -7AM

You increase the time to 2 hours a day

PRAYER WARRIOR LEVEL

MIDNIGHT PRAYERS

DAYS	PRAYER TIME	PRAYER TIME
MONDAY	5AM -7AM	12AM -2AM
TUESDAY	5AM -7AM	12AM -2AM
WEDNESDAY	5AM -7AM	12AM -2AM
THURSDAY	5AM -7AM	12AM -2AM
FRIDAY	5AM -7AM	12AM -2AM

Midnight prayers are the best. If you are a prayer warrior, you must pray at midnight. This is because the day starts at midnight and not when you wake up. It is at midnight that someone's destiny can be exchanged. Evil spirits can steal your destiny and exchange it with a bad one. This usually takes place at a young age. This is why you are not just a parent because you gave birth to a child or you got someone pregnant. You should also be the first spiritual overseer for your child. You should be someone that is constantly praying for your child's destiny. The prayers you prayed for your child while they were little plays out into adulthood. Demons do their dirt from midnight to 3 am. So, to counter it, you have to pray at midnight. You don't do it for six months and stop. This does not mean you pray every day at midnight, but you find time to do it at least once or twice a week. It has to be a lifestyle. Don't expect things within a certain period. Don't set time for God. Be patient and develop the habit.

NEXT LEVEL –SEASONED PEOPLE

You start praying without limit from 3 hours to 6 hours and you graduate into a retreat. A retreat is when you dedicate a whole day to spending time with God. There are no phones, and no dialogue with people. It is just you and God. You will develop the habit of the secret place. It is a place where you go to meet God. The place where after you have prayed for hours, you wait on God by sitting quiet and waiting for Him to speak. Yes, waiting for God is a habit to develop. You just sit there and wait until He speaks. And God will be speaking, but maybe not the first day or the second day. He might try to see how serious you are. He will surely speak if you don't quit. It is at this level that you start learning what season you are in. Your season will help you to concentrate on a particular thing. If you are in a season of sowing, you can concentrate on that. There are seasons in your life where God will say, "Wait on Me." In this season, study to show yourself approved. In this season, there are no arguments with people, etc. There is always a season in your life. When the spirit reveals it, it helps you to concentrate on a particular mission. There are also instances where you pray 4 to 5 times a day without doing it consecutively. One hour here, 30 minutes there, 45 minutes there, another hour, etc. You are engaging in the realm of prayer. Many times, God will reveal certain things to you or through a prophet, but you have to enforce the Word to bring it to pass. If not, you might never see it come to pass. The enemy will steal the Word from you. Learn to enforce what God says about you through prayers.

How To Stay Out of Jail-God's Way

CHAPTER 15: DREAM DAILY

Dreaming, in this case, is learning to picture the result you want. It will work if you are trying to get out of jail. Start picturing yourself getting out of jail. As you do this, your soul will keep negotiating for your release. All of a sudden one day, your soul will inform your mind. Your mind will locate your body and get you of jail. It sounds like a fairytale, but it works. Remember, you started by reading the Bible, praying, and now you are dreaming. You have no idea how powerful this is until you start doing it. It will change your life. When you repeatedly place a picture of what you want in your mind after prayers have been made it will trigger changes to begin in your life. Learn to engage the pictures of what you want daily. You will find yourself going there as you fall asleep. You are involving the supernatural to change the natural. In this kingdom, you can change anything if you believe. The only issue is whether it will happen immediately or later according to the time God allocated. Martin Luther King said, "I have a dream that my four little children will one day live in a nation where they will not be judged by the color of their skin but the content of their character". He didn't live to see it, but it happened. It came to pass. You can manifest events in your life by repeatedly imagining the picture of that dream. The more you do it, the more it becomes a reality.

CHAPTER 16: NOW THAT YOU ARE OUT OF JAIL

What are you going to do? Are you going to stop reading and praying? No, you continue the same regimen and continue to grow in your spiritual life. You need to analyze why you were in jail and make changes in your life. Change the people around you, especially if you are experiencing peer pressure. Don't allow friends to continue getting you in trouble. It is time to make changes to make sure you don't end up in the same place. Remove yourself from the environment if you have to. Find a church home to go to. Attend regular church services and learn more about God. There are many aspects of God that you are yet to learn. Find out what you are called to do. Why are you here on earth, and what will God have you to do? To find out what your calling is, you have to follow your gift. Whatever you are gifted in will lead you to your calling.

Your gift is what comes very easy to you and you enjoy doing it. You will do it for free and have so much joy doing it. That is your gift. A gift is not a hobby. You can get tired of a hobby and pick up another one. You cannot live without your gift; it is part of who you are. It is like the air you breathe. Take an active role in church. Pay attention to see where your gift can be used in Church. Church leadership will usually ask you where you would love to serve. Join a division in the church, whether it be the choir, security team, usher, hospitality host, prayer team, etc. Whatever you feel that you can do, go ahead and be a part of that group. Constantly engaging in church activities will keep you honest and out of trouble.

    Learn how a Godly person behaves daily. Learn what it entails to work with God every day. Learn what your church home expects from you. Surround yourself with people who want to get better. These are people to hold you accountable. Very often people are disenchanted with going to church because of an individual's behavior. As you go to church, please do not allow an individual to cause you to stop going. This is a trick by the enemy. Maintain a consistent church-going habit, and understand that you are going there to hear from God, and not man. For example, if two people are sitting in a church service listening to the same sermon, they could hear different things from the same sermon. God will often use a sermon to talk to you about your situation. He will speak to your point of need without the speaker being aware of it. Church can be a supernatural experience. You go with expectancy, not to look at people and their behavior, but to hear from God. People today argue about everything in the church, from praises and worship, to tithing. I believe in all of it.

Tithing is Biblical so make sure you tithe. Stay away from the misconception that you should not tithe. Or better yet don't think that Pastors are taking the money. Do you know how hard it is to be a Pastor? Trust me even if you were paid, it is extremely hard to do. You cannot do it without God's help. Ignore people looking for something to talk about. Tithing is primarily used to take care of the house of God. So then, you and I could go there to hear the gospel free of charge. Without tithing, most churches would be closed. It takes care of the house of God first before the Pastor. Of course, there are people out of here taking advantage of it. But you do your part and honor God. So His work will continue on the earth, and you let God deal with the pastor.

CHAPTER 17: WHERE ARE YOU?

Your destiny is looking for you, searching everywhere for you, but when it finds you, will she recognize you? Joseph's destiny was waiting for him in Egypt. He had the dream. Then he told his brothers and his father Jacob about it. The brothers thought they were punishing him by selling him into slavery but they were pushing him forward into his destiny. When he got to Potiphar's house, he had a problem with the wife trying to sleep with him. He ended up in jail to continue his journey. (Genesis 39). Potiphar had entrusted everything in Jacobs's hand. It will seem as if his life was perfect except for the fact that it wasn't his final destination. He needed to go one step further to attain a position much higher than he had with Potiphar. He couldn't go straight from slavery to Pharaoh's house because he wasn't ready, he wasn't old enough. In the same way, your destiny will only recognize you when you have been processed. You have gone through the stages of your life, and your learning is up to par. If that doesn't happen, you will find yourself going backward to learn from your previous experiences. Always pay attention as to why something happened to you. If you don't, it will keep coming back because you refuse to learn from it. Life journey is set up to prepare you, but the learning is up to you. You can go through the journey, but if you didn't learn anything, it has to be repeated until you learn it. God will never give you a position you are not qualified for. In life, you have to go through training to start a job. In Gods' kingdom, He uses life experiences and your reaction to it to judge what you learned. This will determine what you are qualified to handle. Many are still stuck in middle school in the journey to their destiny because that's where they stop learning. Physically, this individual maybe 35 years' old. However, in God's calendar in destiny, his knowledge is still at middle school level.

At each stage of your life, your destiny expects to meet you there. If you are not there, it will continue to wait for you to get there. The problem is that many will never get there because they took the backroad and it lead them somewhere else. If Joseph never made it to Pharaoh's house, someone else not as capable as Joseph will assume that position and there will be some adjustments in the spirit realm to prepare that individual to handle the position. That individual will never be a Joseph. There will be pain and suffering because the original didn't make it to the promise land. Learn to follow God's path. For, it has incredible rewards. They are more than you think. If your destiny is calling you from Atlanta, Georgia, do not be found wondering in Nashville, Tennessee. There are people you have to impact and in some cases their life is tied to yours. Learn to obey God. Remember, you can only obey God if you learn how He operates. It is impossible to please a God you do not know. It is not realistic for you to find your destiny if you have no idea where you are going. Your destiny is calling you. Can you hear her? She is getting desperate because you keep getting lost. Find your way today. (John 14:6) Jesus said unto him, I am the way, the truth, and the life: no man cometh unto the Father, but by me.

CHAPTER 18: REFUSING COUNSEL

I have never seen a generation that refuses to get counsel even from their own parents like this generation. (Proverbs 15:32) He who listens to life-giving reproof will dwell among the wise. He who ignores discipline despises himself, but whoever heeds correction gains understanding. Refusing to listen to counsel shortens the knowledge transfer from one generation to another. Why is knowledge transfer important? Knowledge transfer is important because there is a certain amount of information that has to be transferred to the next generation. It creates continuity, and helps to keep the devil from gaining advantage over us. What you don't know can destroy you. If you didn't know your father used to be an alcoholic, a drug dealer, or a thief, you might not understand where your problem is coming from. Why is your son is behaving the way he is? It is like trying to build a house without laying foundation. Without a solid foundation, that house will not stand. It saves you the headache. The headache of fixing problems when I could have seen it from afar and made sure to stay away from it. If I recognize the problem ahead of time, it will save me the headache. Every generation lays a foundation for the next. You hope that your kids would not go through the same things you did. If I studied architecture in college and I established a business for 20 years in the field, I can transfer the knowledge I have to my son without him having to go to college to learn it. He can now go to college to enhance or add to what he knows already. By doing this, he has a chance to be greater than I was. When you refuse counsel, you are trying to learn things you could have gotten for free. Spending 4 to 5 years to learn and pay for knowledge you could have gotten for free. You can only build a good legacy when young people are willing to learn. Now, your father or mother might be a really difficult person to learn from. Most times it is up to you. I had some difficult lecturers in college. I had no choice but to find out what they expected from me and how to please them. Isn't it amazing that if the same experience plays out with your parent, you will probably quit rather than adjust yourself. There are things your parents know that you are going to need in your life. If you allow them to die with the knowledge, that area of your life will suffer. It might take you years to learn that simple thing you could have gotten had you humbled yourself with your parents.

    This generation will not be okay without knowledge transfer. The reason you read about leaders of the past is to gain knowledge and strength for the future. Learn to receive counsel from those who walked before your time. It will save you a lot of headaches, and a lot of unnecessary pain. Take a look at your life. What advice did you reject in the past that came back to haunt you? Some are paying dearly for their stubbornness. Some will die because they didn't listen. Please pay attention to your life when it comes to counsel. God will send people into your life to help you navigate through life. However, if you refuse to listen you will miss it. You can miss your destiny because you didn't listen. This is all part of being humble. You don't know everything. Stop talking so much and listen. It might save your life. God bless.

CHAPTER 19: INTERCESSOR

We are looking for intercessors. Three different types of intercessor, one group for America, second group for the world at large and the last group for the heavens. Somebody will copy this idea, as it is allowed. We need praying people to pray for America. This country is at the forefront of the Gospel. The impact of America shakes the world. Nothing happens until somebody prays. Prayer will resurrect anything dead, humans and all. I stand in the volume of the book that is written of me, humbly to have this privilege to speak the mysteries of God. Earlier we talked about prayer, an intercessor is different. This is someone who prays as a lifestyle. The second group praying for the world is for a reason. There is something God is doing; he wants to bring together a certain type of people in the world to cause the earth to respond to birth pain according to his will. Let there be illumination as you read, let your eyes open that you can see. He is calling intercessors from every nation to take their place, when you get in position you will have understanding and clarity. Jews pray 3 times a day, Muslims pray 5 times a day. How many times a day do you pray? Something is coming in the kingdom of God, those who pray will be just fine but those who don't will be frustrated and some will kill themselves out of stress. I hear about Pastors killing themselves, I recently had a friend die from a heart attack while waiting to become the Pastor of a church. I pray the enemy will not take you out before your time. There is someone sitting beside you while you are looking for a wife, or for a husband. There is someone who doesn't look the part right now and you are ignoring them because you cannot see. Your husband, your wife is right there but he looks dirty, she stinks and you are ignoring them. You are looking for a ready-made man or women. That is because you are blind. If only you could see, you will know that your blessing is right there. Illumination will bring manifestation from the realms of the spirit to the natural. The next intercessor group prays for the world at large. In every country, God has an agenda. These are people praying for the agenda of God to come to pass in the world. The last groups for heaven, that his will come to pass on earth as it is in heaven (Mathew 6:10). Your kingdom come, your will be done, on earth as it is in heaven.

Nothing happens unless a man prays. These individuals will constantly get their prayer point from heaven. They only pray for heavens agenda. Heaven has an agenda, and it is a place of submission, and of surrender. They are people who are not interested in their personal agenda but only a God Agenda. These individuals are very different, as they don't argue with men.

There was also a prophetess named Anna, the daughter of Phanuel, of the tribe of Asher, who was well along in years. She had been married for seven years, and then was a widow to the age of eighty-four. She never left the temple, but worshipped night and day, fasting and praying. Coming forward at that moment, she gave thanks to God and spoke about the Child to all who were waiting for the redemption of Jerusalem. (Luke 2:38)

    This is the anointing they carry, which is the anointing of prophetess Anna. They are not looking for fame, they don't need to be noticed, or seen but that they are working for God. They pray for men of God who don't know it, and they get their assignment from God. They will be celebrated in heaven.

How To Stay Out of Jail-God's Way

www.ingramcontent.com/pod-product-compliance
Lightning Source LLC
Chambersburg PA
CBHW072023110526
44592CB00012B/1409